blue

bucket

jeans

blueberries

torch

purple

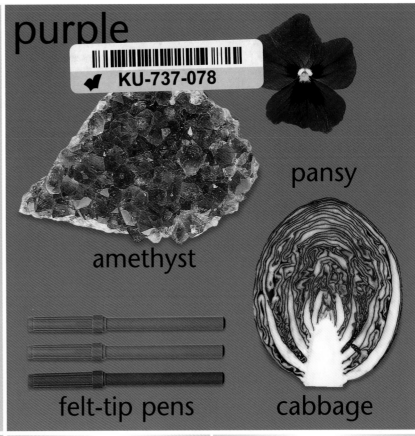

KU-737-078

pansy

amethyst

felt-tip pens

cabbage

grey

toy elephant

brown

fir cone

biscuit

gold

stars

play money

silver

ring

fork

pink

baby lotion

gloves

prawns

toy pig

black

coal

cat

olives

shoes

3

My alphabet

Point to **w** and **z**! Can you spell your name?
Let's say the alphabet together!

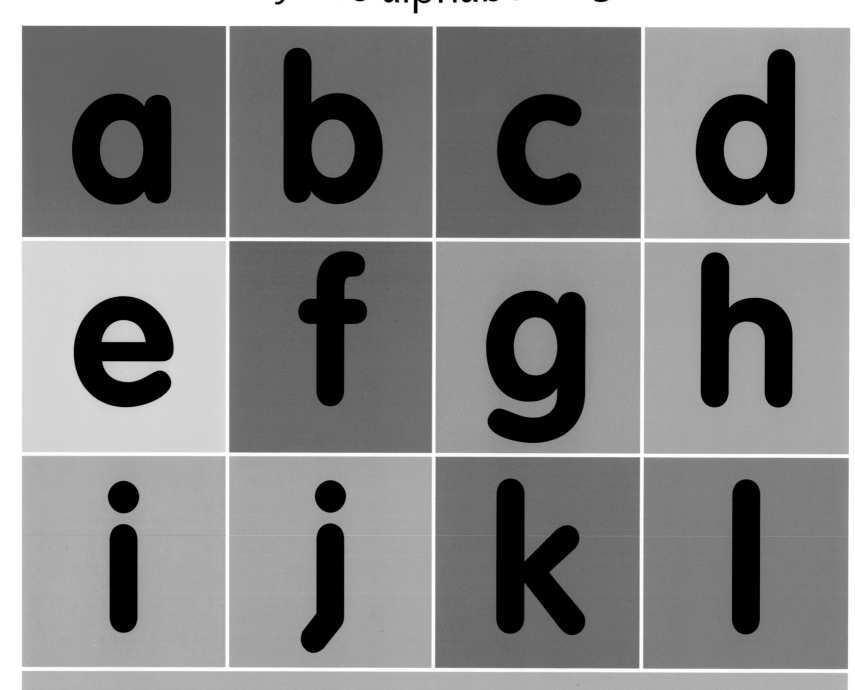

a b c d e f g h i j k l m n o p q r s t u v w x y z

A B C D E F G H I J K L M N O P Q R S T U V W X Y Z

a first book of

words

Chez Picthall

picthall and gunzi

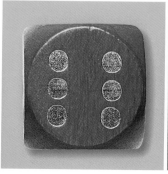

Colours

Which is your favourite colour?
What colours are you wearing today?

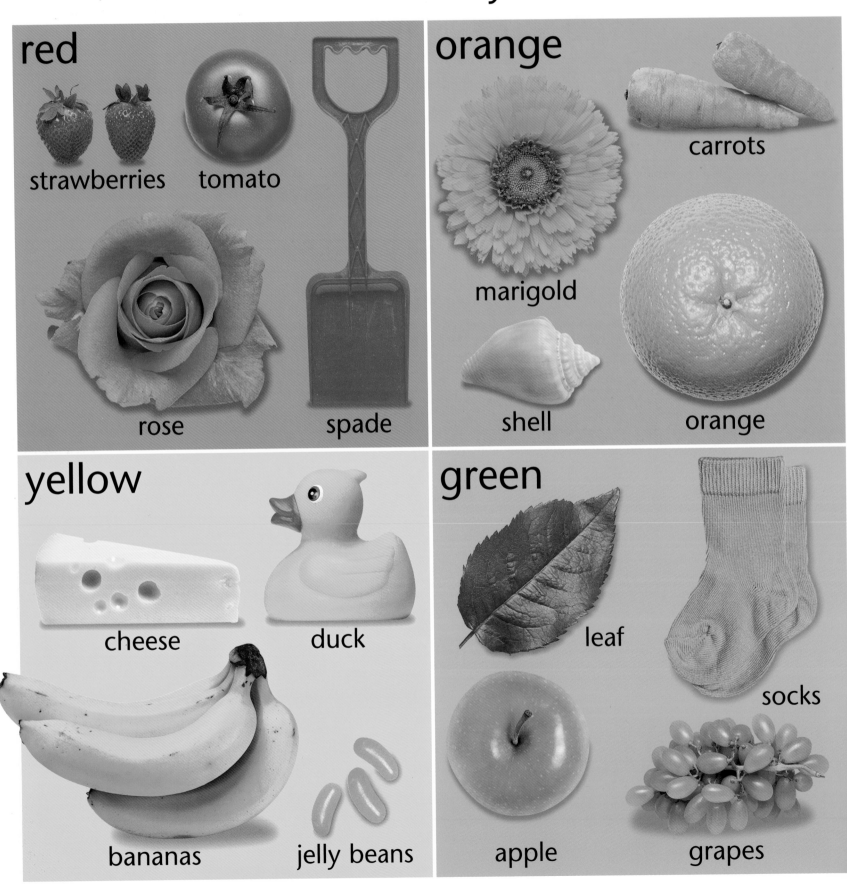

red

strawberries

tomato

rose

spade

orange

carrots

marigold

shell

orange

yellow

cheese

duck

bananas

jelly beans

green

leaf

socks

apple

grapes

m n

o p q r

s t u v

w x y z

A B C D E F G H I J K L M N O P Q R S T U V W X Y Z
a b c d e f g h i j k l m n o p q r s t u v w x y z

Numbers

Let's count to 10!   Point to number seven!
How many cars can you count?

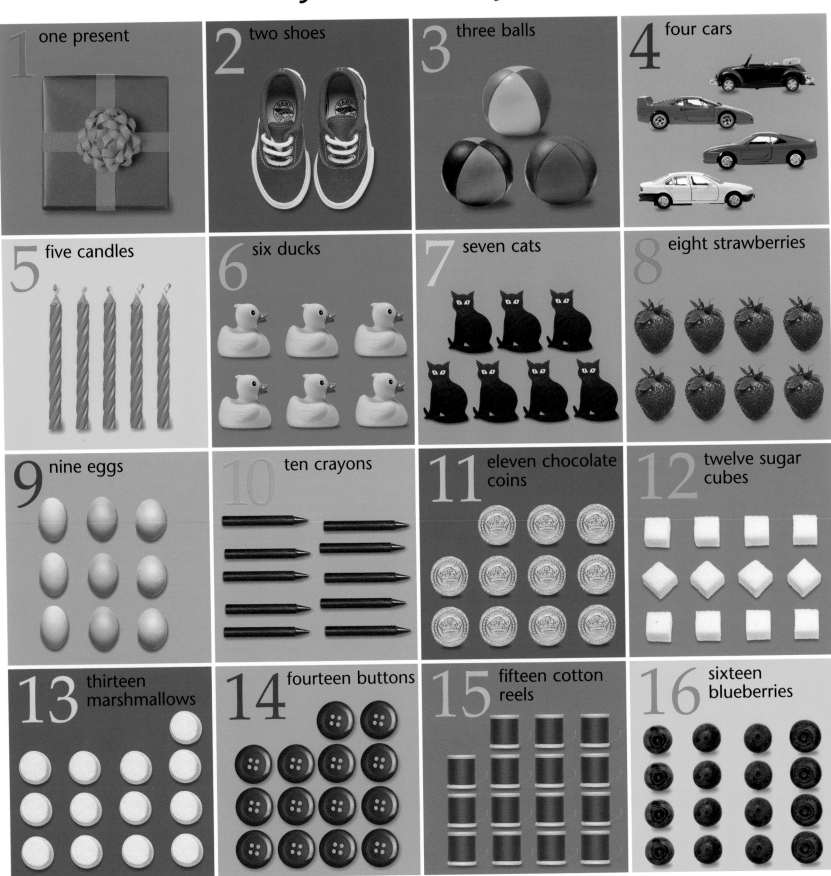

1 one present

2 two shoes

3 three balls

4 four cars

5 five candles

6 six ducks

7 seven cats

8 eight strawberries

9 nine eggs

10 ten crayons

11 eleven chocolate coins

12 twelve sugar cubes

13 thirteen marshmallows

14 fourteen buttons

15 fifteen cotton reels

16 sixteen blueberries

17 seventeen beads

18 eighteen sweets

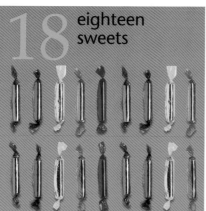

19 nineteen pencil sharpeners

twenty stars

30 thirty shells

40 forty biscuits

50 fifty flowers

My body

Let's clap our hands! Can you find the eyes?
Which parts of the body do you know?

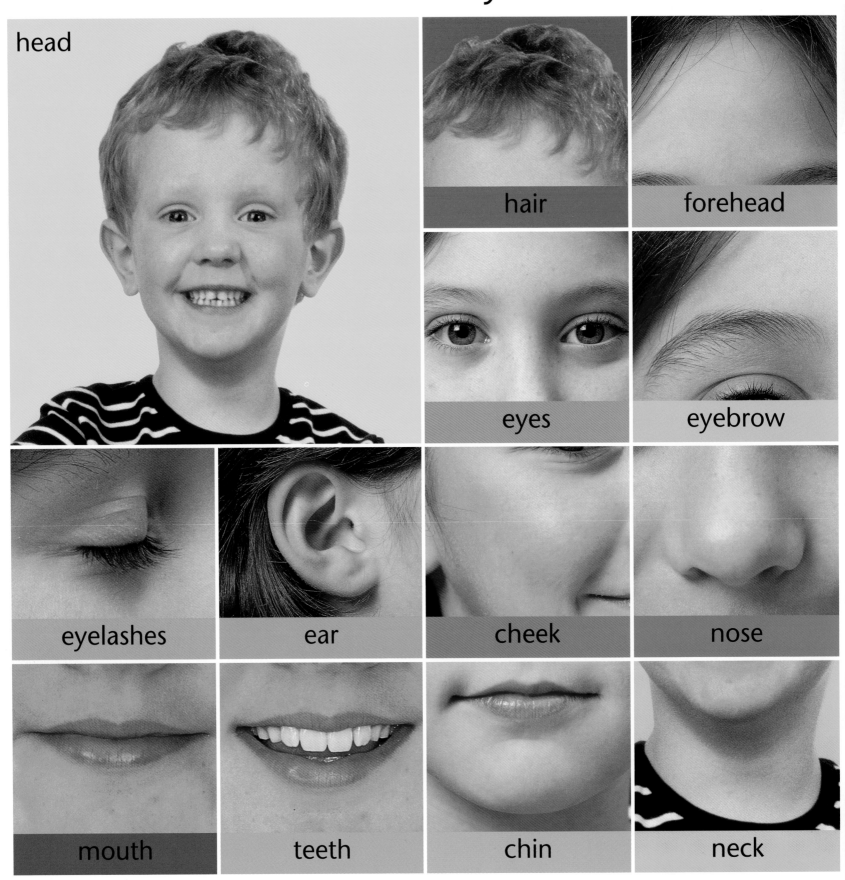

head

hair

forehead

eyes

eyebrow

eyelashes

ear

cheek

nose

mouth

teeth

chin

neck

8

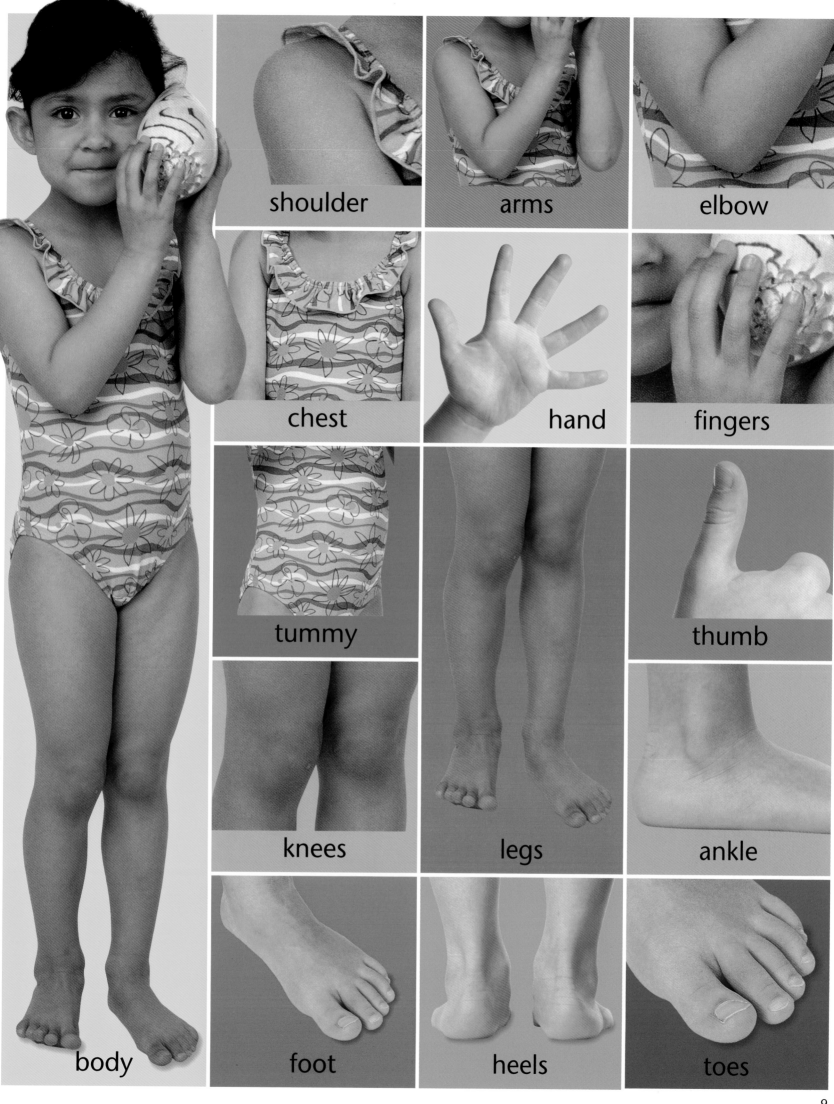

shoulder

arms

elbow

chest

hand

fingers

tummy

thumb

knees

legs

ankle

body

foot

heels

toes

What we wear

What do you wear when it's cold?
What are you wearing today?

raincoat

sleep suit

bib

cardigan

dungarees

shoes

vest

knickers

jeans

pants

socks

coat

tie

jacket

canvas shoes

trousers

dress

baseball cap

skirt

T-shirt

boots

shirt

belt

scarf

jumper

mittens

wellingtons

gloves

woolly hat

tights

In the kitchen

What do you like to make?   Find four pans!

Can you see some things to eat?

plate

saucepan

spatula

salt and pepper

eggs

whisk

flour

baking tin

pastry cutters

oven gloves

fridge freezer

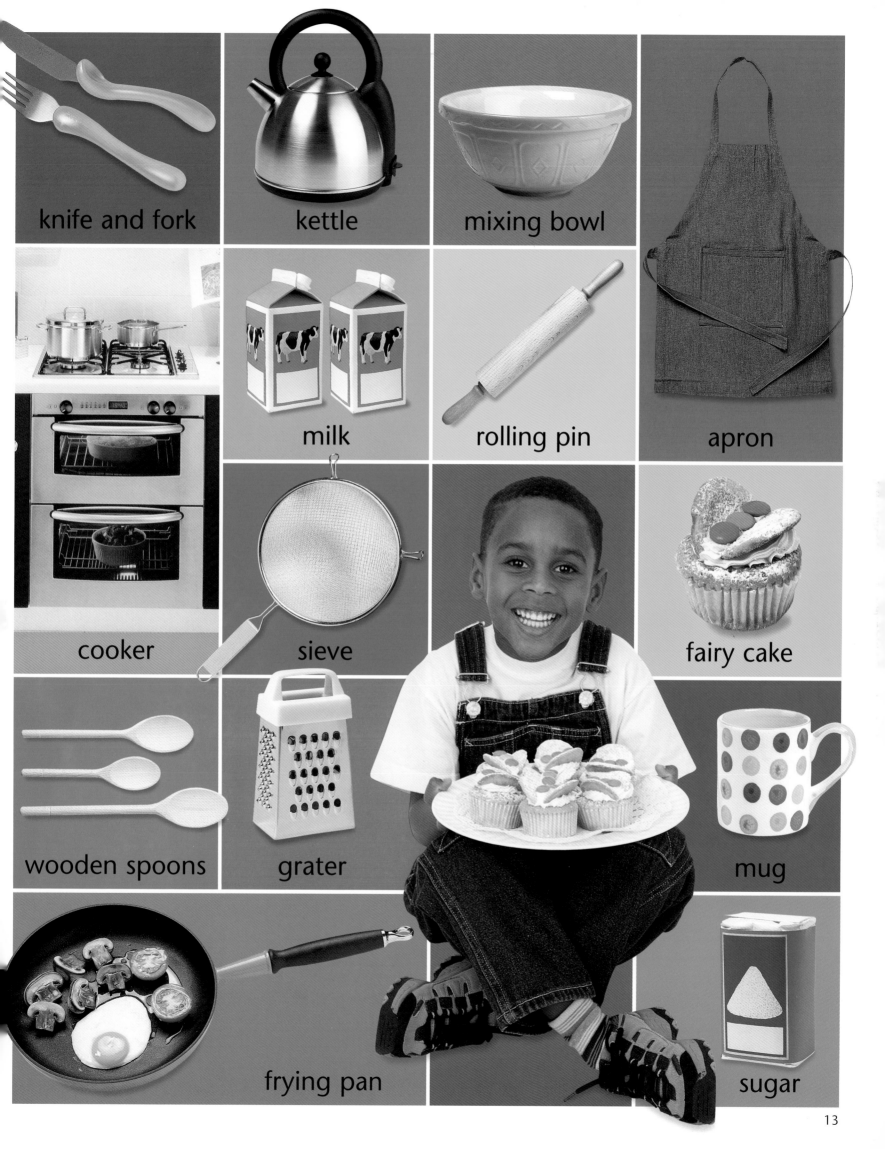

knife and fork

kettle

mixing bowl

apron

cooker

milk

rolling pin

sieve

fairy cake

wooden spoons

grater

mug

frying pan

sugar

What we eat and drink

Which of these foods do we eat hot?

What do you like to eat?

sandwich

pasta

cereal

milkshake

sausages

baked beans

popcorn

yogurt

pizza

bagel

fruit salad

baked potato

hamburger

cheese on toast

apple pie

boiled eggs

waffles and syrup

salad

bread

stir-fry

biscuits

orange juice

chips

muffins

crisps

quiche

ice cream

doughnut

chicken

Fruit

Point to the pears! Let's find all the red fruit! Which is your favourite fruit?

pineapple

strawberries

peaches

cherries

bananas

pears

blueberries

oranges

plums

kiwi fruits

lemons

grapes

melon

apples

raspberries

mango

Vegetables

Name all the vegetables! Find the potatoes!

Count the green vegetables!

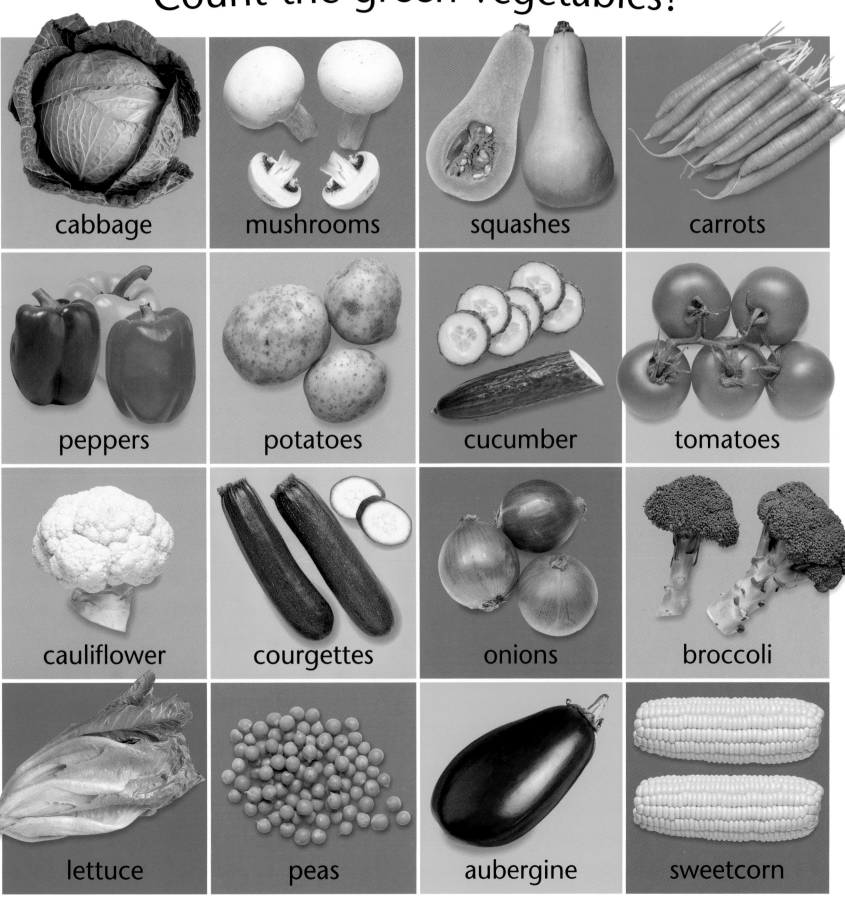

cabbage

mushrooms

squashes

carrots

peppers

potatoes

cucumber

tomatoes

cauliflower

courgettes

onions

broccoli

lettuce

peas

aubergine

sweetcorn

Playtime

Let's name the toys! Which toys make music? Can you find a dinosaur?

cuddly toys

marbles

drum

modelling clay

spinning top

skipping rope

masks

aeroplane

puzzle

robot

lorry

toy spring

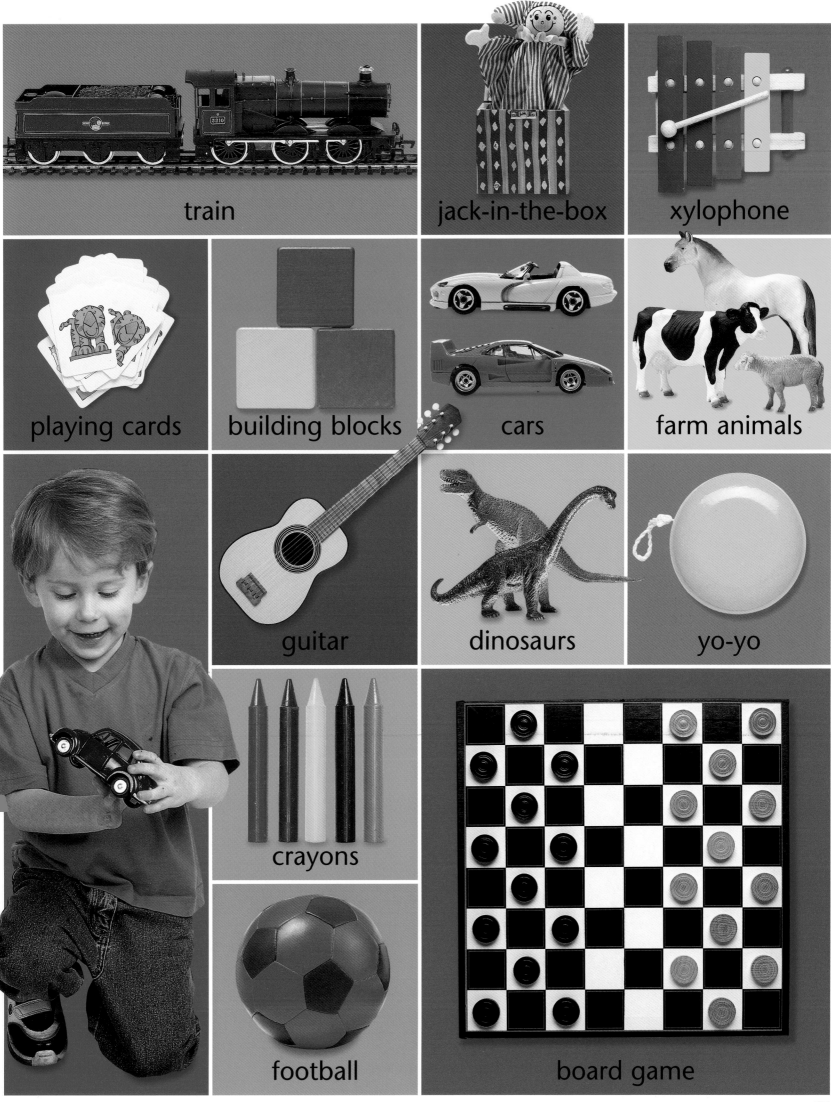

train

jack-in-the-box

xylophone

playing cards

building blocks

cars

farm animals

guitar

dinosaurs

yo-yo

crayons

football

board game

Bathtime

Point to the potty!   What is in the bath?

What do you use to clean your teeth?

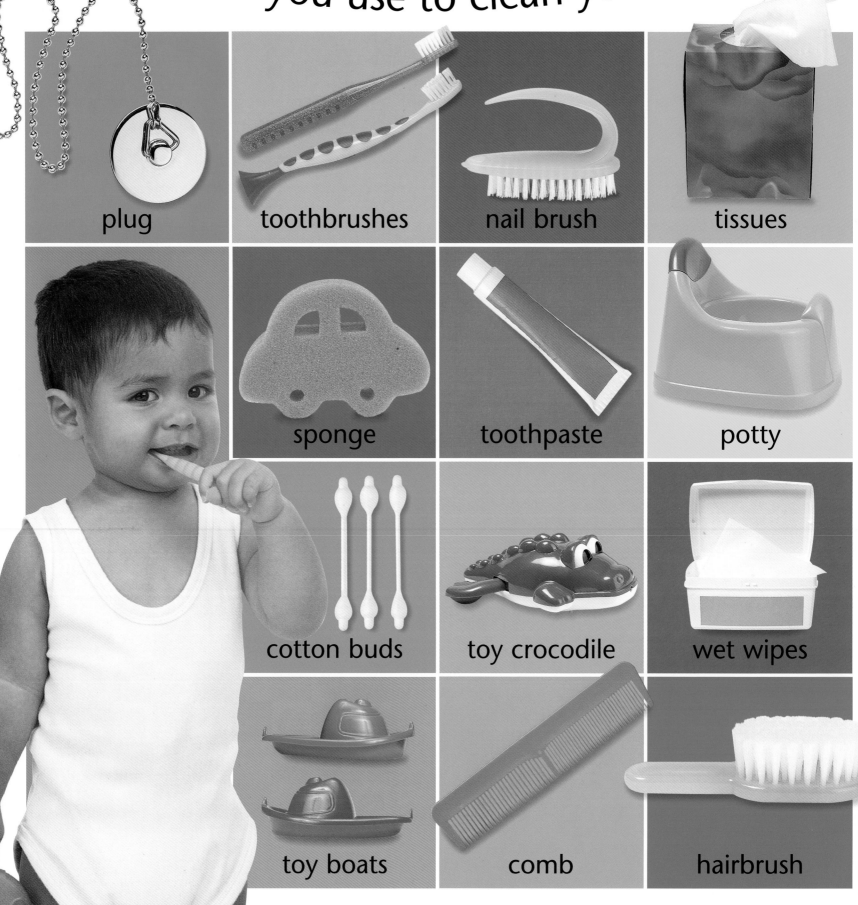

plug

toothbrushes

nail brush

tissues

sponge

toothpaste

potty

cotton buds

toy crocodile

wet wipes

toy boats

comb

hairbrush

talcum powder

shampoo

cottonwool balls

toy duck

face cloths

soap

tap

toilet paper

towels

bubble bath

bath

wash basin

Bedtime

What do you wear in bed?   Find the duvet!

How many slippers can you count?

moon

glow stars

lamp

teddy bears

pyjamas

blankets

beaker

slippers

hot-water bottle

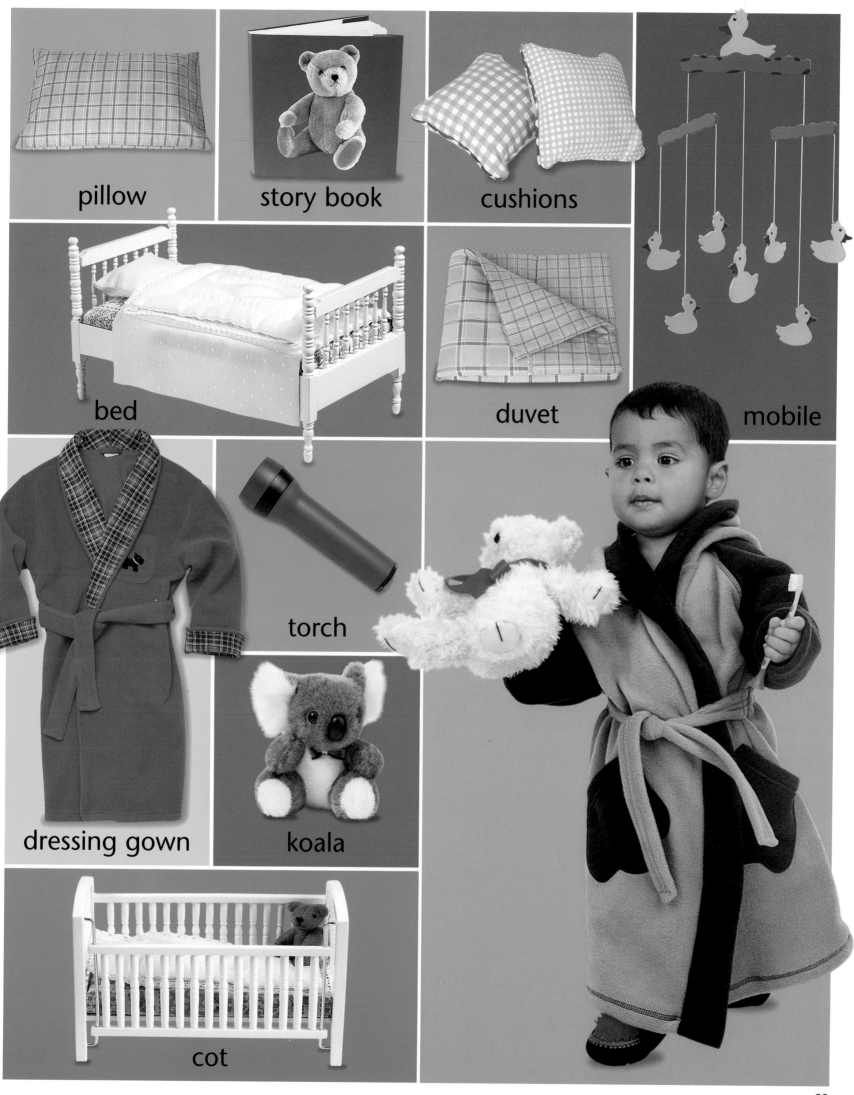

pillow

story book

cushions

bed

duvet

mobile

torch

dressing gown

koala

cot

At school

Point to the letters! Count the children!
Which things do you use for drawing?

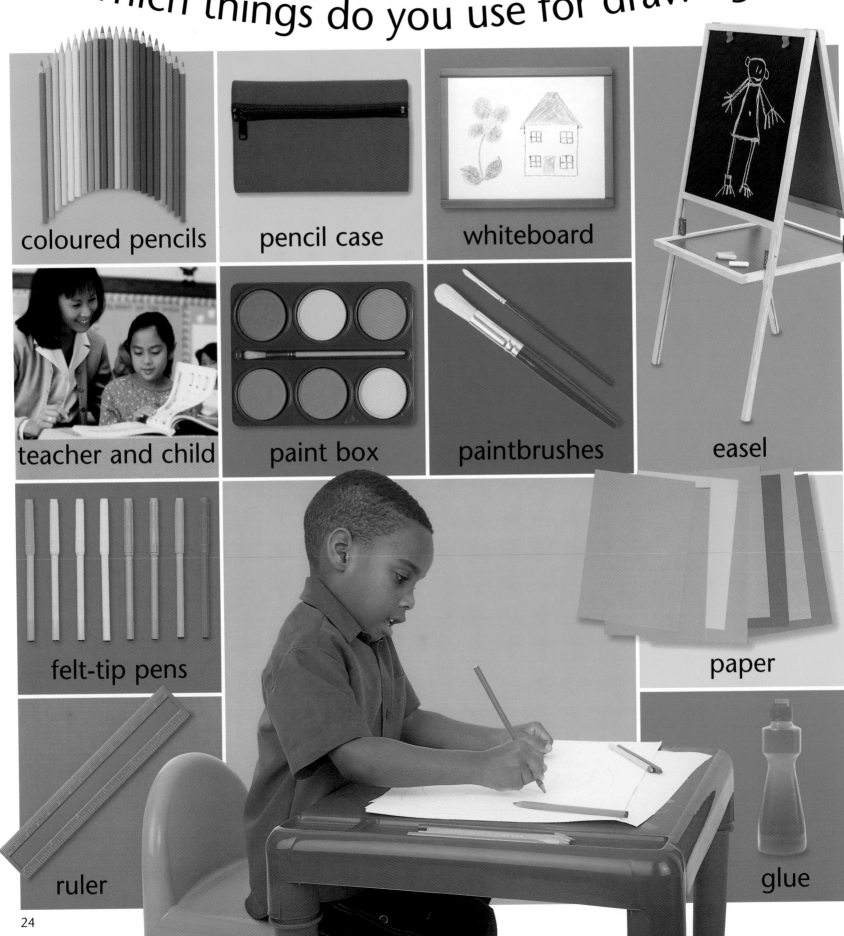

coloured pencils

pencil case

whiteboard

teacher and child

paint box

paintbrushes

easel

felt-tip pens

paper

ruler

glue

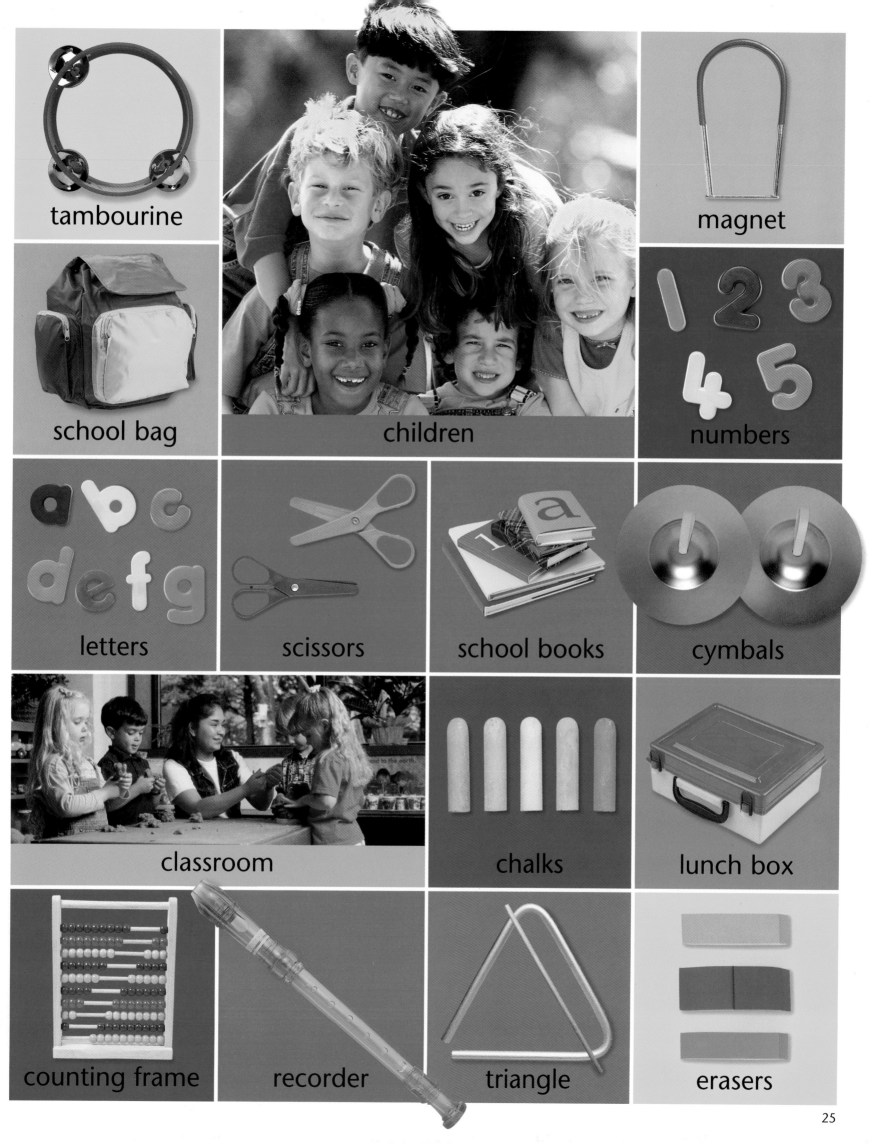

tambourine

school bag

children

magnet

numbers

letters

scissors

school books

cymbals

classroom

chalks

lunch box

counting frame

recorder

triangle

erasers

25

On the move

Let's name these together! Count all the cars!
Can you see some things that fly?

airship

hang-glider

transporter

train

mountain bike

car

yacht

fire engine

ferry

motorbike

ambulance

taxis

speedboats

jumbo jet

hot-air balloon

helicopter

parachute

aeroplane

monorail

space shuttle

supersonic jet

delivery van

tram

school bus

ship

police car

racing car

In the countryside

Let's name the animals! Point to the flowers!
What can you see in the countryside?

mouse

dandelions

owl

leaves

ants

grasshopper

ferns

fox

stream

tree

daisies

acorns

centipede

bluebell woods

bee

bridge

woodpecker

berries

buttercups

squirrel

meadow

conkers

rabbit

dragonfly

bird's nest

fir cone

toadstools

toad

lane

caterpillar

twigs

waterfall

On the farm

Let's count the ducks!

What grows in an orchard?

What machines can you see?

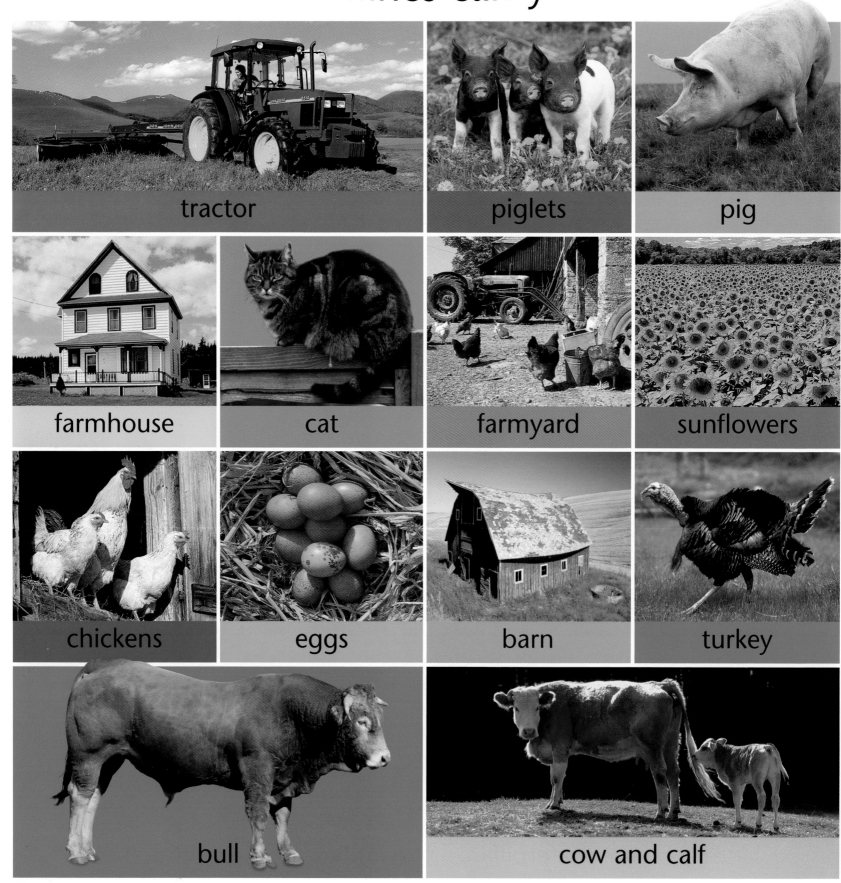

tractor

piglets

pig

farmhouse

cat

farmyard

sunflowers

chickens

eggs

barn

turkey

bull

cow and calf

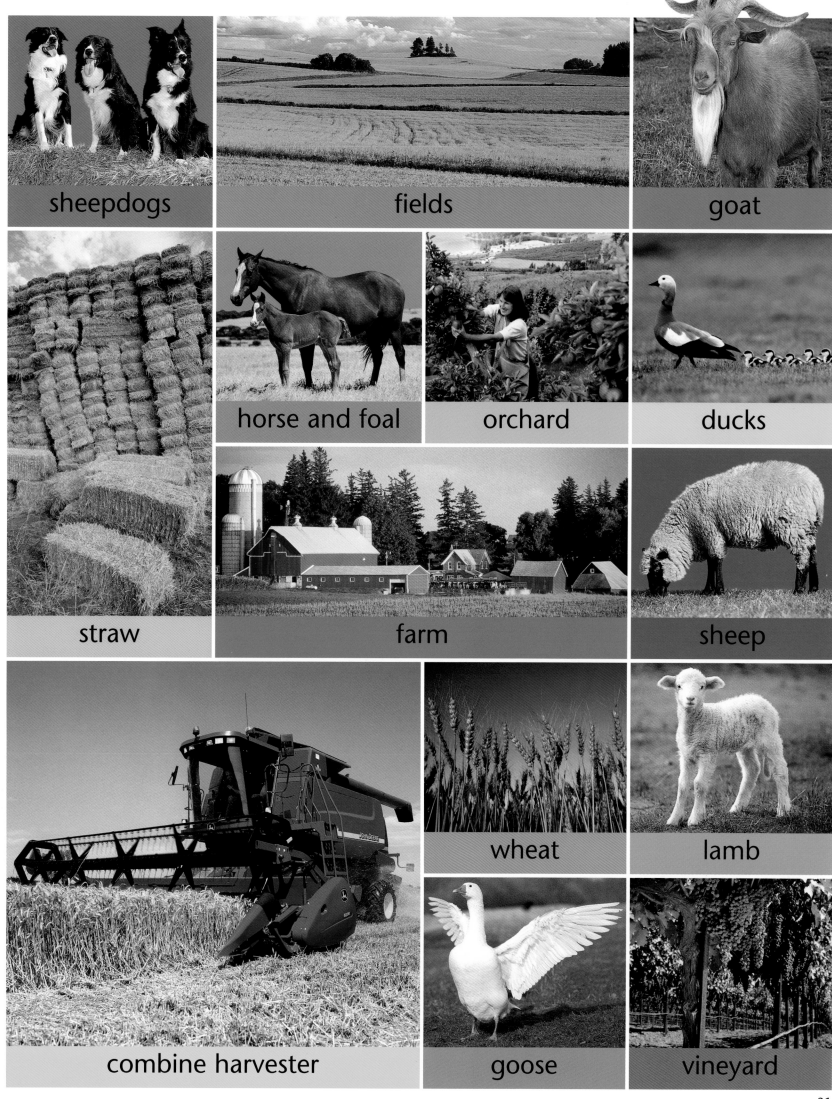

sheepdogs

fields

goat

straw

horse and foal

orchard

ducks

farm

sheep

combine harvester

wheat

lamb

goose

vineyard

Time

What time is it now? Can you find the moon?
Let's say the numbers on the clock!

sunrise

day

sun

breakfast time

teatime

lunch time

clock

bedtime

sunset

night

moon